Understanding Planetary Placements

Sophia Mason

Copyright 1993 by American Federation of Astrologers, Inc.
All rights reserved.
No part of this book may be reproduced or transmitted in any form or by any means, electronic or mechanical, including photocopying or recording, or by any information storage and retrieval system, without written permission from the author and publisher. Requests and inquiries may be mailed to: American Federation of Astrologers, Inc., PO Box 22040, Tempe, AZ 85285-2040.

Current Revised Printing: 1993
ISBN: 0-86690-365-8

Published by:
American Federation of Astrologers, Inc.
PO Box 22040
6535 S. Rural Road
Tempe, AZ 85285-2040

Printed in the United States of America

Books by Sophia Mason

Forecasting With New, Full and Quarter Moons
Basic Fundamentals of the Natal Chart
Aspects Between Signs
Understanding Planetary Placements
Lunations and Predictions
The Art of Forecasting
Delineation of Progressions
From One House To Another

Contents

Understanding Planetary Placements	1
Sun's Role in the Universe	3
Moon's Role in the Universe	9
Mercury's Role in the Universe	15
Venus's Role in the Universe	27
Mars' Role in the Universe	39
Jupiter's Role in the Universe	45
Saturn's Role in the Universe	53
Uranus' Role in the Universe	63
Neptune's Role in the Universe	71
Pluto's Role in the Universe	79

Understanding Planetary Placements

Many budding astrologers have experienced at one time or another a feeling of frustration and despair over the vast amount of information they feel they have to learn or memorize, or the numerous books that must be read before they can grasp the knowledge and the workings of astrology. By learning the basic foundations of planetary rulership and applying them to their natural signs or houses, the task of chart delineation is so much easier.

For example, the list under the Sun holds true for fifth house matters as well as Leo. The Sun basically rules children, love affairs and conditions of the heart; so do Leo and the fifth house. At the end of every planetary list are several examples for applying them to houses, signs and aspects.

It is my sincere hope that this book will be assistance in helping others make the transition from novice astrologer to professional.

It is also my desire that this book help eliminate the need to memorize phrases or statements written by other authors merely because students feel they do not have the potential to describe these planetary placements in their own words.

Everyone has a distinct style of writing and speaking. Keep your statements simple and direct, and you will come across with far more sincerity. Believe me.

Sextiles and Trines
Sophia Mason

Sun's Role in the Universe

The Sun is ruler of the fifth house and the sign Leo, which falls between the period of July 23 and August 22 and is symbolized by the Lion.

It takes one year for the Sun to make a complete transit through the 12 signs of the zodiac, traveling at the rate of one sign per month or approximately one degree per day.

The Sun's nature is fixed, fiery, hot, dry, masculine and moderately fruitful.

The **Sun** is **exalted** in **Aries**
Has its **fall** in **Libra**
Is in its **detriment** in **Aquarius**

Favorable Aspects

Favorable aspects to the Sun include **sextiles** and **trines** to all the planets, as well as **conjunctions** and **parallels** with Mercury, Venus and Jupiter.

Unfavorable Aspects

Unfavorable aspects to the Sun include **squares** and **oppositions** to all the planets as well as **conjunctions** and **parallels** with Mars, Saturn and Uranus.

Doubtful Aspects

Doubtful aspects to the Sun include **conjunctions** and **parallels** with the Moon, Neptune or Pluto, which can be good or bad depending on whether the aspects received from other planets are favorable or unfavorable.

Mental and Emotional Attributes and General Characteristics

Favorably Aspected	Unfavorably Aspected
Affectionate	Animalistic
AMbitious	Arrogant
Ardent	Boastful
Authoirty	Commanding
Charitable	Conceited
Confident	Dictatorial
Cooperative	Disdainful
Creative	Domineering
Dignified	Egotistical
Dynamic	Glory seeking
Encouraging	Haughty
Faithful	Lack of ambition
Flamboyant	Lack of confidence
Generous	Overbearing
Gracious	Showy
Honorable	Stubborn
Influential	Subtle cruelty
Leadership ability	Tyrannical
Loyal	Vain
Nobility	
Optimistic	
Organizational ability	
Popularity	
Power	
Pride	
Respectful	
Strong willed	
Superiority	
Vitality	
Well mannered	

People and Things

People
Actor
Administrator
Advertising agent
Chairmen
Children
Employer
Executive position
Foremen
Important official
Jeweler
King
Leader
Managerial position
Men of authority
Men aged 35 to 45
Proud and haughty person
Queen
Superior

In a female's chart, the father in early life; then the vocational position or the husband in adulthood

Things
Advancement
Amusement park
Ballroom
Creativity
Entertainment
Exhibit
Position
Disgrace
Dishonor
Fairs and fairgrounds
Fame
Fine wine
Fire
Gambling
Game
General prosperity
Gift
Glory
Gold
Government affairs
Grandeur
Grant
Health
Honor
Individuality
Item of quality
Lavish furnishings
Lion
Parks and playgrounds
Publicity
Royalty
Romance
Speculation
Social affair
Sunday
Theater

Health
Arteries
Back
Circulation of the blood
Constitution
Afflictions of the eyes such as cataracts or glaucoma
Fevers
Energy
Heart
Heart disease and ailments
Inflammation
Left eye of the female
Right eye of the male
Spine and spinal column
Sunburn
Sunstroke
Vitality

Applying the Planetary Position of the Sun, Leo and the Fifth House

If, for example, Leo is on the cusp of the second house of money, one may wonder which word to choose from the listing under the Sun. This is a simple matter: use any word as long as it is applied in terms of money, moveable possessions and sociability because Venus is the natural ruler of this house. Also choose words from the favorable and unfavorable lists because transiting planets in the second house under the sign Leo will be influenced by various aspects.

As an example, refer to the first column under General Characteristics.

The native will be ambitious when it comes to earning personal income. He will be charitable and generous to the financial needs of others. Now, switch to the second column. However, he should guard against the tendency to be somewhat showy or boastful with personal possessions for as can be seen in the list under Things, there is an attraction to items of quality and lavish furnishings. Glancing through the next two columns of People and Things, note that children and romance will have some influence on personal finances (much depends upon the aspects to the natal Sun in the native's chart).

The native may desire a managerial position through which he earns his or her money.

Applying the list to an aspect, for example the Sun trine Pluto. Pluto is a complex planet to understand, but this list should make it a bit easier. Because of the trine, use the first column under General Characteristics for both the Sun and Pluto and combine them.

First, both the Sun and Pluto are of a fixed nature because they are governed by the fixed signs Leo and Scorpio. The emotions would be deep and intense.

In the first column for the Sun, note the words affectionate, ardent and faithful, and in the first column for Pluto, there is fierce possessiveness and intense loyalty. These individuals would not enter into a love affair lightly; instead, there would be a strong sense of loyalty and devotion regarding the relationship.

Suppose Pluto were in the fifth house in Cancer and the Sun in the ninth house in Scorpio. The native would have some kind of creative (fifth house) talent that would interest the common people (Pluto in Cancer).

And, in trine aspect with the Sun in Scorpio in the ninth house, higher education might be necessary to fulfill this promise or he might be interested in research (Sun in Scorpio) involving writing or publications (Sun in the ninth house). Many Scorpios have been known to express themselves in a somewhat sarcastic manner. But, with the Sun in the ninth house, it will pick up some of the coloring of Jupiter, the natural ruler of that house. Thus there is more of a charitable, benevolent and compassionate concern with the social welfare of others (all these words were taken from the first column of Jupiter).

If one of the planets, perhaps the Sun, were in the tenth house and trining Pluto in Cancer in the sixth house of service, it might instill a strong interest in the medical field. Sun in Scorpio in the tenth house falls under Saturn's coloring and this native would be very ambitious and desirous of holding a position of responsibility and trust, preferably a vocation where he can be his own boss.

Scorpio is strongly interested in surgery and the medical field, as is Pluto especially when in Virgo. Note the words doctor, hygienist and healer.

With Pluto in Cancer in the sixth house, there may be an interest in the reproductive organs (Cancer) and matters to do with birth and death (Sun in Scorpio). These factors could be the makings of a gynecologist or surgeon.

However, it is important to look further into the natal chart to confirm findings. Does the ninth house indicate higher education, and in what possible fields? What sign is on the Ascendant and where and in what sign is the ruler located? All this will help determine the native's vocational interest and potential for growth.

Moon's Role in the Universe

The Moon is the ruler of the fourth house and Cancer, which falls between June 21 and July 22 and is symbolized by the crab.

It takes one month for the Moon to make a complete transit through all 12 signs of the zodiac at the rate of two and a half days in each sign and traveling approximately 13 degrees per day.

The Moon's nature is cardinal, watery, cold, moist, feminine and fruitful.

The Moon is **exalted** in **Taurus**
Has its **fall** in **Scorpio**
Is in its **detriment** in **Capricorn**

Favorable Aspects

Favorable aspects to the Moon include **sextiles** and **trines** to all planets as well as **conjunctions** and **parallels** with Mercury, Venus, and Jupiter.

Unfavorable Aspects

Unfavorable aspects to the Moon include **squares** and **oppositions** to all the planets as well as **conjunctions** and **parallels** with Mars, Saturn and Uranus.

Doubtful Aspects

Doubtful apsects to the Moon include **conjunctions** and **parallels** with the Sun, Neptune and Pluto, which can be good or bad depending on whether the aspects they receive from other planets are favorable.

Mental and Emotional Attributes and General Characteristics

Favorably Aspected	Unfavorably Aspected
Adaptable	Anxious concern about money and security
Affectionate	
Agreeable	Becomes easily overwrought
Benevolent	Carping
Cautious	Complainer
Dependable	Constnat need of affection
Domestic	Clannish
Economical	Daydreamer
Emotional sensitivity	Dependent upon others
Emotional perception	Dwells on past events and slights from others
Excellent memory	
Feeling	Expands hurt feelings out of proportion
Fertile imagination	
Gentle	Emotional depression
Industrious	Emotional vulnerability
Impressionable	False impressions
Intuitive	Fantasizes to escape from reality
Kind	Fear of ridicule, rejection and criticism
Loving	
Maternal instinct	Fickle
Mediumistic	Fretfulness
Modest	Greedy
Patriotic	Hyper-sensitive
Paternal instinct	Inconstant
Personal magnetism	Inhibited
Protective	Indecisive
Psychic ability	Insecure
Quiet	Irritable
Receptive	Mistrusts others
Reserved	Martyr
Resourceful	Melancholy
Security minded	Miserly
Sensitive	Moody

Favorably Aspected
Sentimental
Sympathetic
Tenacious
Traditional
Trustworthy

Unfavorably Aspected
Nagger
Overly protective, romantic and sentimental
Passive
Pessimistic
Potential for self pity
Quiet
Retiring
Restless
Requires emotional reassurance
Sensationalism
Sensuality
Secretive
Suspicious
Sloppy
Self sacrificing
Self delusive
Self protective
Tenacious
Touchy
Uncommunicative
Unforgiving
Unstable
Unwarranted fears, worries and anxieties

People and Things

People
Antique dealer
Baby
Babysitter
Baker
Boat builder
Beverage maker
Bartender
Businessman
Chef

Things
Bathing
Beach
Beer
Beverage
Boats
Brewery
Change
Domestic affairs
Emotions

People	Things
Cocktail waitress	Evening
Cook	Environment
Caretaker	Fishing industry
Custodian	Glass and bottles
Chemist	Groceries and food
Coin collector	Harbor
Crowd	Health
Dairyman	Home and residence
Dressmaker	Hotel
Emotional people	House trailer
Family	Imagination
Female relations	Kitchen
Fisherman	Lakes and water
Forester	Land and real estate
General public	Laundry
Grandmother	Love of country
Gourmet cooks	Liquid
Governess	Lighthouse
Gardener	Magnetism
Historian	Maritime
Home economics teacher	Memory
Homemaker	Monday
Hotelier	Moods
Housekeeper	Navy
Kindergarten teacher	Navigation
Laundry worker	Nutrition
Masses of people	Nursery
Mother	Old age and close of life
Midwife	Personality
Meteorologist	Public
Nurse	Psychic power
Night worker	Restauruant
Night watchman	Shipping industry
Obstetrician	Seashore
Older woman	Subconscious mind
Queen	Tavern
Real estate agent	Voyage

People	Things
Restaurant manager	
Sailor	
Stamp collector	
Traveler	
Wife	
Women in general	

Health
Body fluids
Breasts
Brain
Cancer
Child birth and pregnancy
Conception and childbearing organs
Digestive organs
Dropsy
Emotional disturbances
Flabbiness
Fluid retention
Functional ailments and irregularities
Left eye of the male
Right eye of the female
Menstruation
Ovaries
Stomach disorders
Tumors
Uterus

Applying the Planetary Positions of the Moon, Cancer and the Fourth House

Cancer on the Ascendant (from first column of General Characteristics): The native will have the tendency to be somewhat cautious in his relationship with others for he is very sensitive and emotional. He is endowed with an excellent memory and a fertile imagination, which can be good in the field of creative writing.

The native (from the second column) should not permit himself to dwell on past happenings which he often expands out of proportion, thus making the problem larger than it actually is.

Using the first column under People, Cancers often love to cook and may become gourmet chefs, or work in restaurants (Things). Family relationships play a major role in their lives. From the second column under Things, Cancers are easily influenced by their environment and many have good psychic powers or feelings.

When the Moon is square Saturn, combine the second columns under General Characteristics from the Moon and Saturn lists. Mistrust of others may turn these individuals into opportunists with a single minded drive towards personal achievement above all else, (Saturn). The Moon rules the emotions and the mother, who may have been aloof (Saturn), cold and domineering in her attitude toward the native.

The Moon in the eleventh house and in a woman's chart, instills emotionalism (Moon) toward friends (eleventh house). These natives often try to mother their friends. In a man's chart and favorably aspected, the Moon brings older women who become good friends into his life. Unfavorably aspected, women friends tend to give these individuals trouble. If the Moon is in Taurus, the trouble is through female friends because of money. If the Moon is in Pisces, the trouble is the result of deception or alcoholism.

No matter which house position the Moon may be situated in, merely take any word from a column under the Moon and apply it to the particular house in question. But, due consideration must be given to the Moon's sign placement, for this will color the energy of the Moon. If the Moon is in Aquarius in the fifth house, for example, it would give a male an interest in older women (Moon) but also those of unconventional and unique background (Aquarius).

If the Moon is in Pisces, look under the columns for the Moon and combine them with the columns under Neptune. If it is in the tenth house, look under the columns for the Moon and combine them with the columns under Saturn (natural ruler of the tenth house).

Mercury's Role in the Universe

Mercury is the ruler of the third and sixth houses and governs Gemini and Virgo. Gemini falls between May 21 and June 20 and is symbolized by the Twins. Virgo falls between August 23 and September 22 and is symbolized by the Virgin.

It takes one year for Mercury to make a complete transit through all 12 signs of the zodiac at the rate of one sign per month and varying in travel from 16 degrees to one degree, 24 minutes.

Mercury retrogrades an average of three or four times a year, each period lasting approximately 24 days. The stationary period is approximately one day before and one day after.

Like Venus, Mercury huddles quite close to the Sun and is generally never more than 28 degrees away. Therefore, one can be assured that Mercury will be either in the same sign as the Sun, the sign before or the sign after the Sun.

Mercury's nature is mutable, dualistic, cold, moist, sexless and moderately fruitful. Mercury is a neutral planet and depends solely upon its Sun position, aspects and house location for its energy to manifest itself.

Mercury is **exalted** in **Aquarius**
Has its **fall** in **Leo**
Is in its detriment in **Sagittarius** and **Pisces**

Favorable Aspects

Favorable aspects to Mercury include **sextiles** and **trines** to all the planets as well as **conjunctions** and **parallels** with the Moon, Venus, Sun and Jupiter.

Unfavorable Aspects

Unfavorable aspects to Mercury include squares and oppositions to all the planets as well as conjunctions and parallels with Mars, Saturn and Uranus.

Doubtful Aspects

Doubtful aspects to Mercury include conjunctions and parallels with Neptune and Pluto, which can be good or bad depending on whether the conjunction or parallel receives favorable or unfavorable aspects from other planets.

Mental and Emotional Attributes and General Characteristics (Gemini)

(If Mercury or other planets are positioned in Gemini or the third house, their energies naturally will manifest through the Gemini sign or third house matters disclosed in the following list. Should Mercury be positioned in a house or sign other than Gemini or the third, then both lists from Gemini and Virgo will have to be carefully interpolated.)

Favorably Aspected	Unfavorably Aspected
Ability for logic	Compulsive analysis
Ability to memorize	Aloof
Ability to reason	Anxious
Accuracy	Biting
Active	Bores easily
Adaptable	Brooding
Alertness	Calculating
Ambitious	Changeable
Analytical	Clumsy
Brilliant	Cold
Candid	Coy
Clever	Cunning
Capacity for concentration	Cynical
Charming	Deceitful

Favorably Aspected	**Unfavorably Aspected**
Cheerful	Depressing
Communicative	Dishonest
Creative	Dissatisfied
Courteous	Distrustful
Curious	Easily distracted
Comprehensive	Evasive
Dazzling	Exasperating
Dexterity	Excessive talker
Duality	Excitable
Enterprising	Feelings of inadequacy
Extroverted	Fickle
Flexibile	Foolish
Friendly	Falsehood
Imaginative	Forgetful
Improvisation	Gossip
Ingenious	High strung
Innovative	Hostile
Intellectual	Illiterate
Intuitive	Idle conversationalist
Inventive	Inconsistent
Irresistible	Ignorant
Likes to experiment	Indecisive
Lively	Indiscriminate
Literary ability	Inquisitive
Linguistic ability	Impatient
Magnetic	Intolerant of routine
Mental agility	Insatiable appetite for variety
Mental dexterity	Irritable
Musical	Irrational
Observant	Lacks sincerity in emotional attachments
Oratorical	
Perceptive	Lacks concentration
Persuasive	Lacks continuity
Precise	Melancholic
Precise	Mischievous
Quick witted	Moody
Rational	Narrow minded

Favorably Aspected	Unfavorably Aspected
Shrewd	Nervous
Skillful	Nonconformist
Seeker of fun and pleasure	Omits words or alters meaning
Sensitive	Overactive
Sociable	Petty thievery
Sparkling	Profanity
Versatile	Repetitive
Vivacious	Restless
Witty conversationalist	Resents authority
Witty conversationalist	Sarcastic
	Scatters energy
	Stupid
	Superficial
	Talkative
	Talks excessively about insignificant details
	Tricky

People and Things (Gemini)

(This list applies to those planets positioned in Gemini or the third house. Should Mercury be positioned in a house or sign other than Gemini or the third, then lists from Gemini and Virgo must be carefully interpolated.)

People	Things
Ad writer	Automobile
Agent	Accident
Ambassador	Bicycle
Artist	Book
Automobile mechanic	Bus
Bookbinder	Bus station
Bookkeeper	Communication through conversation, letter, mail, messenger and telephone
Bicycle dealer and repairman	
Brother	
Bus driver	Changes in the immediate environment and neighborhood
Businessman	
Business machine repairman	Contract
Businessman	Desk

People
Cab driver
Chauffeur
Child
Clerk
Commentator
Cousin
Craftsman
Critic
Debaters
Dock worker
Editors
Educator
Elevator operator
File clerk
Gossiper
Handwriting expert
Inspector
Journalist
Lecturer
Librarian
Linguist
Literary agent
Mail carrier
Manicurist
Mechanical engineer
Mechanic
Messenger
Motorcyclist and repairman
Neighbor
Newspaper carrier
Newspaper reporter
Photoengraver
Porter
Printer
Proofreader
Professional traveler
Radio broadcaster and operator

Things
Everyday acquaintance
Filing cabinet
Gossip
Hand gesture
Idea
Schools (primary and secondary)
Short trip
Streetcar
Thought
Traffic control
Transportation
Typewriter
Library
Literature
Magazine
Mail
Market place
Memory
Mentality
Motorcycle
News
Newspaper
Post office
Periodical
Power of perception
Print shop
Published material
Railroad yard
Road
Rumors
Studies
Written document

People	Things
Railroad employee	
Salesman	
Secretary	
Schoolmate	
Scientist	
Service station attendant	
Shipping and receiving clerk	
Sister	
Speaker	
Stenographer	
Student	
Teacher	
Teenager	
Telephone installer and repairman	
Telephone solicitor	
Ticket agent	
Translator	
Traffic control worker	
Travel agent	
Truck driver	
Typesetter	
Typist	
TV announcers and operators	
Visitor	
Writer	
Young people	

Health (Gemini)
Ailments and accidents to the arms, hands and shoulders
Asthma
Bronchitis
Bronchial tube
Collar bone
Coordination
Emphysema
Larynx
Lung disease and disorders

Mental faculties and disorders
Nervous illness and conditions due to stress and worry
Nervous system
Nervous temperament
Pleurisy
Pneumonia
Psychological problems
Pulmonary problems
Reflexes
Respiratory problems
Speech impediment
Sensory nerves
Sense of touch, smell and hearing
Thyroid

Mental and Emotional Attributes and General Characteristics (Virgo)

(If Mercury or any other planets are positioned in Virgo or the sixth house, their energies will naturally manifest through the Virgo sign or sixth house matters. Should Mercury be positioned in a house or sign other than Virgo or the sixth, lists from Gemini and Virgo must be carefully interpolated.)

Favorably Aspected	Unfavorably Aspected
Accurate	Careless
Adaptable	Carping
Alert	Changeable
Analytical	Complainer
Assimilative	Critical
Calm	Demanding perfection of others
Capacity for concentration	Dependent on others yet wants to be in control of them
Cautious	
Chaste	Discontented
Considerate	Deceitful
Conscientious	Delusions of persecution
Contemplative	Easily confused
Cultured	Exacting to a fault
Cool	Fault finding
Deals with facts	Fear of criticism

Favorably Aspected	Unfavorably Aspected
Dependable	Finicky
Detail minded	Fussy
Dexterity	Hardness of character
Devoted	Hoarder
Deep sensitivity	Hypercritical
Discriminating	Hypersensitive
Efficient	Hypochondria
Exacting	Impatient with others
Faithful	Impractical
Fastidious	Inconsistent
Hard worker	Indecisive
Helpful	Introverted
Honorable	Lack of coordination
Humility	Loner
Hygienic	Manipulative
Idealistic	Nagger
Imaginative	Narrow minded
Industrious	Nervous
Intellectual	Overly solicitous
Literary ability	Overly critical
Mentally active	Overly concerned with details
Methodical	Overly fastidious
Meticulous	Paranoid
Modest	Phobia or fear of germs and contamination
Neat	
Objective	Phobia or fear of disease and ill persons
Observing	
Orderly	Restless
Painstaking	Shy
Perfectionistic	Slow witted
Poised	Superficial
Practical	Stupid
Precise	Susceptible to flattery
Protective	Trics to control others by being overly solicitous
Quiet	
Reliable	Underhanded
Reserved	Unfeeling

Favorably Aspected	Unfavorably Aspected
Scientific	Worrier
Self reliant	Worries about the reaction of others
Shrewdness of character	Wasteful of energy and time
Sincere	
Studious	
Strongly ingrained habits	
Sympathy and compassion	
Trustworthy	
Unassuming	
Unbiased	
Unselfish	
Versatile	
Very selective	
Virtuous	
Works well alone	

People and Things (Virgo)

(This list applies to those planets positioned in Virgo or the sixth house. Should Mercury be positioned in a house or sign other than Virgo or the sixth, both lists from Gemini and Virgo must be carefully interpolated.)

People	Things
Administrator	Agency
Accountant	Armed forces
Agriculturist	Cafeterias
Animal trainer or breeder	Clothing
Administrator of nursing home	Diet
Aunt	Disappointment
Analytical scientist	Food
Analytical chemist	Grocery store
Bank teller	Health
Appraiser	Health food
Bookkeeper	Hygiene
Brokerage	Hiring of employees
Businessman	Illness
Chemist	Medicine
Clerk	Nutrition

People
Co-worker
Critic
Critical people
Data processor
Dental hygienist
Dietician
Doctor
Draftsman
Druggist
Dry cleaner
Dental technician
Efficiency expert
Farmer
File clerk
Fire fighter
Food inspector
Gardener
Healer
Hygienist
Inferior person
Journalist
Laboratory technician
Librarian
Mathematician
Medical stenographer
Merchandise manager
Nurse
Office manager
Osteopath
Pharmacy
Police officer
Programmer
Salesman
School principal
Scientist
Secretary
Service repairman

Things
Peace Corps
Personal hygiene
Produce market
Public works
Red Cross
Restaurant
Small pet
Vitamins
Work in general
Working condition

People	Things
Servant	
Statistician	
Teacher	
Tenant	
Uncle	
Veterinarian	

Health (Virgo)
Abdominal region
Appendicitis
Bowels and bowel disorder
Digestive tract
Hypochondria
Indigestion
Intestines
Intestinal disorder
Mental stress which reacts on the stomach causing acidity, colitis, constipation, dyspepsia, diarrhea
Nervous temperament
Personal hygiene
Skin conditions, eruptions and psoriasis resulting from nervous tension
Tuberculosis
Ulcers

Applying the Planetary Positions of Mercury, Gemini and Virgo, and the Third and Sixth Houses

The lists under Mercury and Saturn can be used for Mercury in Capricorn, Mercury in aspect with Saturn or Mercuryn in the tenth house.

Depending upon the house position, Mercury in Capricorn can represent an older (Saturn/Capricorn) brother or sister (Mercury). If Mercury in Capricorn is unfavorably aspected in the natal chart, it can mean the native shoulders responsibilities (Saturn/Capricorn) of the brother or sister (Mercury).

A well aspected Mercury in Capricorn endows depth of thought (Saturn/Capricorn) with good organizational ability and persistence (Saturn/Capricorn) in any studies (Mercury) that interest the native.

Unfavorable aspects to Mercury in Capricorn may instill a tendency towards mental (Mercury) depression (Saturn/Capricorn) and a lack of humor.

Mercury trine Saturn indicates mental (Mercury) control (Saturn/Capricorn) and discipline (Saturn/Capricorn). Speech (Mercury) and actions are well considered (Saturn/Capricorn), for the native uses good common sense.

Mercury square Saturn gives mental (Mercury) backwardness and depression (Saturn/Capricorn), and harbors fears of rejection and failure.

Different words were taken from both columns under Mercury and Saturn and combined. If, for example, Mercury were in the tenth house (irregardless of the sign position), the native might experience this placement as a genuine need to further his studies (Mercury) to acquire a higher career status. However, because the tenth house has an earthy element to its coloring, (Capricorn, natural ruler of the tenth house, is both cardinal and earth), the sign Virgo should be stressed.

Looking at the chart of a teacher who has Mercury positioned in her tenth house, not only would she strive for a master's degree in education, but also have a strong desire to achieve a position of authority (see the Virgo List under People) such as a school principal.

Remember, the tenth house is normally ruled by Saturn and under its list of People are administrators, bosses, executives and those authority.

Venus' Role in the Universe

Venus is ruler of both the second and seventh houses and governs Taurus and Libra. Taurus falls between April 20 and May 20 and is symbolized by the bull. Libra falls between September 23 and October 22 and is symbolized by the scale.

It takes one year for Venus to make a complete transit through all 12 signs of the zodiac at the rate of one sign per month; travel varies from one degree nine minutes to one degree fourteen minutes per day.

Venus retrogrades approximately once every 18 months with the period lasting about 40 days. The stationary period is two days before retrogration and about two days after.

Like Mercury, Venus huddles quite close to the Sun and is generally never more than 48 degrees away. Therefore, one can be assured that Venus will be either in the same sign as the Sun, the sign before or the sign after the Sun sign.

Venus' nature is benefic, warm, moist and fruitful. She is also considered a feminine planet.

    Venus is **exalted** in **Pisces**
    Has its **fall** in **Virgo**
    Is in its **detriment** in **Aries** and **Scorpio**

Favorable Aspects

Favorable aspects to Venus include **sextiles** and **trines** to all planets as well as **conjunctions** and **parallels** with the Moon, Mercury, Sun, Jupiter and Neptune.

Unfavorable Aspects

Unfavorable aspects to Venus include **squares** and **oppositions** to all planets as well as **conjunctions** and **parallels** with Mars, Saturn and Uranus.

Doubtful Aspects

Doubtful aspects to Venus include **conjunctions** and **parallels** with Pluto, which can be good or bad depending on whether the conjunctions andrallels receive favorable or unfavorable aspects from other planets.

Mental and Emotional Attributes and General Characteristics (Taurus)

If Venus or any of the other planets are positioned in Taurus or the second house, their energies will naturally manifest through Taurus or second house matters as listed. Should Venus be positioned in a house or sign other than Taurus or the second, lists from Taurus and Libra must be carefully interpolated.

Favorably Aspected	Unfavorably Aspected
Agreeable	A bore
Affectionate	Aloof
Appreciative of quality	Assaultive and destructive temper
Ardent	Demanding
Artistic	Dislikes change
Cautious	Difficult to understand or approach
Calm	
Composed	Difficult to communicate with
Careful	Easily upset by change
Compassionate	Emotional and material insecurity
Concentrative	Fears loss of prestige and possessions
Conservative	
Creative	Fear and resistance to change
Dogmatic	Fixed in ideas and opinions
Dependability	Furious and violent in temper
Determination	Greedy
Devoted	Hard
Endurance	Hostile

Favorably Aspected	**Unfavorably Aspected**
Faithful	Hypersensitive
Firm	Immovable
Generous	Inertia
Good taste	Indolent
Gentle	Indulgent
Graciousness	Irrationally stubborn and obstinate
Helpful	Jealous
Hospitable	
Hard worker	
Integrity	
Kind	
Level headed	
Love of beauty, luxury and comfort	
Loyal	
Meticulous	
Modest	
Motivated to accumulate monetary and material possessions	
Musical	
Patient	
Peaceful	
Persistent	
Planner	
Pleasant disposition	
Practical	
Protective	
Productive	
Quiet	
Reliable	
Retiring	
Rigid	
Refined	
Slow to anger	
Secretive	
Security minded	
Solid	

Favorably Aspected	Unfavorably Aspected
Soft spoken	
Sensitive	
Self disciplined	
Self restraint	
Slow to form opinions	
Suppresses display of emotions	
Stability	
Strength	
Strong will power	
Well mannered	

People and Things (Taurus)

This list applies to those planets positioned in Taurus or the second house. Should Venus be in a house or sign other than Taurus or the second, then lists from Taurus and Libra must be carefully interpolated.

People	Things
Architect	Artistic pursuits
Aartist	Bank
Banker	Bank book
Bank teller	Cash register
Beautician	Beauty shop
Builder	Check book
Businessman	Comfort
Cabinet maker	Farms and farming implements
Carpet installer	Female occupations
Cashiers	Food
Commercial artist	Flowers
Cook	Loan
Dancer	Money
Dietician	Moveable possessions
Domestic relations counselor	Music
Farmer	Purse
Financier	Safe
Florist	Sculpture
Geologists	Securities
Horticulturist	Strong box

People
Industrial designer
Landscaper
Nurse
Sales agent
Social worker
Sculptor
Singer
Surveyor
Teacher
Therapist
Treasurer

Things
Trunk
Vault
Wallet
Wealth

Health (Taurus)
Cerebellum
Croup
Ears
Goiter
Larynx
Laryngitis
Lymphatic system
Mumps
Neck
Palate
Pharynx
Tonsils
Throat ailments and infections
Thyroid gland
Vocal cords

Mental and Emotional Attributes and General Characteristics (Libra)

If Venus or any other planets is positioned in Libra or the seventh house, their energies will naturally manifest through Libra or the seventh house matters listed in this chapter. Should Venus be positioned in a house or sign other than Libra or the seventh, lists from Libra and Taurus must be carefully interpolated.

Favorably Aspected
Ability to see both sides

Unfavorably Aspected
Cops out when difficulties arise

Favorably Aspected	Unfavorably Aspected
of an issue	Adulterous
Active	Amorous
Affectionate	Argumentative
Amiable	Changeable and scattered forces
Appealing	Compulsive eater
Artistic	Deceitful
Charming	Dependence on others
Cheerful	Desires attention
Compassionate	Difficulty in facing the
Compromising	hardness or reality of life
Considerate	Discontent
Cooperative	Dislikes anything unpleasant or heav
Courageous	Dominates others
Courteous	Egomaniac
Creative	Emotionally unbalanced
Cultured	Easily led and influenced by others
Desirous of peace at any cost	Fear of isolation and of being
Dislikes argument	or having to live alone
Dignity	Fear of loneliness
Diplomacy	Fickle
Emotional	Flighty
Even tempered	Flirtatious
Extroverted	Frivolous
Excellent host or hostess	Gaudy
Fair	Gullible
Friendly	Indifferent
Fun loving	Indolent
Generous	Indecisive
Gentle	Lack of confidence
Good humored	Love of flattery
Good judgment	Loud
Good promoter	Materialistic
Graceful	Manipulation of others
Gracious	Moody
Gregarious	Narcissistic self love
Harmonious	Need for constant ego bolstering
Idealistic	Over anxious in desire to

Favorably Aspected	**Unfavorably Aspected**
Impartial	please others
Impeccable taste	Overindulge in pleasure
Intellectual	Overly dramatic
Interested in cultural pursuits	Relationships a stepping stone to personal gain
Just	Retreats form reality when life becomes unbearable
Kind	Resentful
Loyal	Selfish
Likeable	Self indulgent
Love of beauty	Self delusion creates life of fantasy
Love of elegance	Self centered
Loving	Superficial
Modest	Susceptible to praise and flattery
Musical	Vain
Neat	Wants things done his way
Need for companionship	
Optimistic	
Outgoing	
Optimistic	
Outgoing	
Perfection	
Persuasive	
Polished	
Poised	
Refined	
Romantic	
Sincere	
Social relations essential to happiness	
Sociable	
Sympathetic	
Sensitive	
Suave	
Tactful	
Talented	
Warm	
Well balanced	
Well mannered	

People and Things (Libra)

This list would applies to those planets positioned in Libra or the seventh house. Should Venus be positioned in a house or sign other than Libra or the seventh, lists from Taurus and Libra must be carefully interpolated.

People	Things
Art dealer	Artistic pursuits
Artists	Art object
Architect	Beauty shop
Beautician	Bedroom
Business partner	Candy
Clothier	Clothing
Clothing designer	Courtship
Confectioner	Dating
Cosmetician	Fur
Counselor	Female occupations
Dancer	Flowers
Decorator	Garden
Dressmaker	Jewelry
Diplomat	Jewelry store
Entertainer	Happiness
Fashion designer	Interior decorating
Fashion model	Love affair
Fur designers and furriers	Luxurious item
Female relation	marriage
Engineer	Party
Florist	Pleasure
Haberdasher	Restaurant
Host and hostess	Romance
Interior decorator	Sexual intrigue
Judge	Sexual intercourse
Labor conciliator	Shopping
Lawyer	Social engagement
Literary critic	Sweet cake
Marriage partner	
Matchmaker	
Mediator	
Milliner	

People	Things
Musician	
Nephew	
Niece	
Opposite sex	
Painter	
Politician	
Playwright	
Poet	
Receptionist	
Salesman	
Sister	
Sweetheart	
Tailor	
TV and movie actors	
Welfare worker	
Wig makers and setters	
Workers and designers of jewelry	
Young woman	

Health (Libra)
Blood clot
Circulation
Diabetes
Diaphragm
Generative system
Sexual organs
Kidneys
Bladder
Lumbar region
Ovaries
Skin disorders
Veins
Venous blood
Urinary tract

Applying the Planetary Positions of Venus, Taurus and Libra, and the Second and Seventh Houses

A well aspected Venus in Aries in the third house would lean more to the Libra list under General Characteristics because the third house has a mutable, airy overtone (Gemini) and Libra is cardinal and air.

Looking under the Libra list, note the words charming, considerate, courteous and refined. Under the Aries list note the words bold, compelling, forceful and frank in manner.

Because the third house (listed under Mercury/Gemini) rules communication, these individuals would be forceful and compelling in their mannerisms, but they would be colored with the energy of Venus. Thus, communication would be handled in such a charming, refined way that there would be no resentment. This would be a very good placement for a diplomat who must be assertive and courteous at the same time.

With natal Venus trine natal Uranus (combining Libra and Uranus) the native is endowed with a magnetic, charming and appealing personality.

Selecting a few words from the column under Things reveals that Libra rules love affairs and pleasure while Uranus is associated with romance and the unconventional. This native would be strongly attracted to unconventional romantic partners or relationships. An unexpected (Uranus) marriage (Venus) may occur if the natal chart holds further testimony to that fact.

Venus trine natal Saturn holds a far different coloring than the Venus/Uranus aspect. Using the same words from the Libra column as used above but with the first column under Saturn, note that there is more reserve, strength and self control. The native would still be charming and appealing, but in a more refined, stable manner without the magnetism of the Venus/Uranus trine.

With Venus in the tenth house, the native would be well liked by bosses and those in authority (Saturn/tenth house) because of the warmth and cheerful attitude shown towards them (Venus). However, the emotions of Venus would still be somewhat reserved and controlled because of the Saturian coloring of the tenth house.

With Taurus on the ninth house, one's personal money might be involved in a legal matter; good or bad depends upon the aspects to natal Venus, ruler of the ninth house; aspects to Jupiter, the natural ruler of the ninth house; and any planets positioned in the ninth house. Money might be gained through in-laws (ninth house) or spent on higher education and travels.

The native with Libra on the eighth house prefers that all sexual activities be treated romantically with gentleness and refinement.

Mars' Role in the Universe

Mars is ruler of the first house and Aries and co-ruler of the eighth house and Scorpio. Aries falls between March 20 and April 19 and is symbolized by the ram.

It takes approximately two and one half years for Mars to travel through all 12 signs of the zodiac at the rate of a little more than two months per sign, varying in travel from one minute to 40 minutes per day.

Mars retrogrades every two years for approximately 80 days., and is stationary about two or three days before and after retrogration.

Mars' nature is cardinal, fiery, hot, dry, masculine and barren.

Mars is **exalted** in **Capricorn**
Has its **fall** in **Cancer**
Is in its **detriment** in **Libra**

Favorable Aspects

Favorable aspects to Mars include **sextiles** and **trines** with all the planets. No conjunction or parallel aspect with Mars is considered favorable.

Unfavorable Aspects

Unfavorable aspects to Mars include **squares** and **oppositions** to all planets as well as **conjunctions** and **parallels** with all planets.

Mental and Emotional Attributes and General Characteristics

If Mars or any other planet is ositioned in Aries or the first house, its energies will naturally manifest through Aries or the first house matters disclosed in the lists below.

Favorable Aspects	Unfavorable Aspects
Active	Abusive
Adventurous	Accepts others at face value
Affectionate	Acts or speaks without forethought
Alert	
Ambitiont	Aggravating
Ardent	Aggressive
Assertive	Anger
Athletic ability	Antagonistic
Bravery	Arrogant
Bold	Boastful
Capable	Bossy
Charm	Bully
Clear thinking	Brutality
Compelling	Combative
Competitive	Conceited
Constructive	Cruel
Creative	Defiant
Courageous	Destructive
Daring	Disruptive
Decisive	Dislikes routine
Defender of the underdog	Domineering
Dignity	Egoism
Direct	Ego needs constant bolstering
Dynamic	Exaggerates
Eagerness	Extravagant
Energetic	Fear of failure and rejection
Enterprising	Foolhardy
Enthusiastic	Feuds
Exciting	Foolish lack of fear
Executive ability	Forceful
Extroverted	Headstrong
Fearless	Hasty

Favorable Aspects	**Unfavorable Aspects**
Forceful	Hot tempered
Frank	Intolerant
Generous	Impatient
Good promotor	Impetus
Idealistic	Impulsive
Industrious	Jealous
Independent	Lacks determination
Inspirational	Lacks emotionsl stability and maturity
Initiative	
Intuitive	Lacks sympathy and consideration for the feelings of others
Inventive	
Kind	Lacks good judgment and sound reasoning
Leadership ability	
Needs freedom of expression	Lustful
Needs and desires recognition or admiration from others	Needs constant stimulation to maintain interest
Optimistic	Needs self discipline
Outgoing	Opinionated
Passionate	Overestimates ability
Pioneering spirit	Outspoken
Positive	Overbearing
Quick	Overly optimistic
Quick to grasp new ideas	Passionate
Quick perception	Pride interferes with sense of values
Resourceful action	
Self assurance	Quarrelsome
Strong	Rebels against authority
Supportive	Rash
Venturesome	Reckless
Victorious	Resentful
Vitality	Rude
Warm	Troublesome
	Self centered
	Self willed
	Tyrannical
	Tries to achieve success by force of action

Favorably Aspected	Unfavorably Aspected
	Uncooperative
	Violent
	Warlike

People and Things

People	Things
Advertising agent	Anger
Assailant	Army
Athlete	Artillery
Baker	Accident
Barber	Auto factory
Builder	Auto repair
Burglar	Auto service station
Butcher	Battlefield
Carpenter	Boiling water
Chemist	Cannon
Construction worker	Cutlery
Craftsman	Danger
Dentist	Death
Engineer	Drills
Executive	Contentions
Fighter	Explosives
Fire fighter	Fire
General	Fireworks
Gunner	Foundriy
Guard	Gun
Hardware salesman	Hardware
Hoodlum	Hurt
Iron worker	Inflammable liquid
Jailor	Injury
Journalist	Iron
Locksmith	Items made of iron and steel
Lumberjack	Knife
Machinist	Machine shop
Male relations	Machinery
Men aged 25 to 35	Molten metal
Metal worker	Operating room

People
Mechanic
Millitary personnel
Molester
Metallurgical engineer
Optometrist
Publicity agent
Police officer
Rival
Robber
Soldier
Surgeon
Salesman
Sheet metal worker
Statesman
Surgical nurse
Teacher
Technician
Tool designer
Veteran
Writer
Welder

Things
Quarrel
New project
New enterprise
Operation
Rape
Rifle
Scald
Scar
Steel
Surgery
Strife
Surgical instrument
Toll
Tool room
Torture
War
Weapon of war
Wound
Wreck

Health
Accident
Allergy
Burns, bruises and blisters
Contagious disease
Cut
Bladder infections and ailments
Face injury
Gall bladder
Head
Headache
Head injuries and scars on the head
High fever
Inflammation
Eyes

Kidneys
Measles
Muscles and the muscular system
Nose
Nervousness
Senses of feeling, sight and taste
Sharp or accute pains and aches
Sinus
Scars and scalds
Surgical operation
Veneral disease
Virility
Wound

Applying the Planetary Positions to Aries and the First House

With Mars in the first house, for example, with aspects to it of mixed influence (good and bad), the individual will be energetic, optimistic and independent. However, because of the unfavorable aspects, there will be a tendency to be aggressiveness, impatience with others and shortness of temper.

Checking the list under Health, Mars is accident prone and may have a scar or blemish on the head or face. Because the first house is a controlling factor regarding health, the native may have high fevers or headaches due to allergies and sinus conditions.

With Aries placed on the second house of money, the motivational force behind this sign is up to the individual himself and how he applies this Arian energy toward personal income. Any word from the lists under Mars can be applied to the second house of money. The native will be enterprising and quick to grasp new ideas when it comes to personal earnings, but should guard against extravagance and impulsive spending. Money may have to be spent on mechanical instruments or tools that may be important to his work.

When Mars (male) is trine the Sun (ruler of children), a male child is almost always promised. Characteristically, in a male's chart, this aspect endows much virility, energy and excellent athletic ability. Leadership ability and a desire to hold a position of authority are prominent.

Jupiter's Role in the Universe

Jupiter is the ruler of the ninth house and Sagittarius and also co-ruler of the twelfth house and Pisces. Sagittarius falls between November 22 and December 21 and is symbolized by the archer.

It takes approximately 12 years for Jupiter to travel through the 12 signs of the zodiac. It spends approximately one year in each sign, traveling between two and three degrees per month.

Jupiter retrogrades for four months and the stationary period is approximately five days before and five days after.

Jupiter's nature is mutable, fiery, hot, moist, masculine and fruitful.

Jupiter is **exalted** in **Cancer**
Has its **fall** in **Capricorn**
Is in its **detriment** in **Gemini** and **Virgo**

Favorable Aspects

Favorable aspects to Jupiter include **sextiles** and **trines** with **all planets,** as well as **conjunctions** and **parallels** with the Moon, Mercury, Venus, Sun and Neptune.

Unfavorable Aspects

Unfavorable aspects to Jupiter include **squares** and **oppositions** to **all planets,** as well as **conjunctions** and **parallels** with Mars, Saturn and Uranus.

Doubtful Aspects

Between Jupiter and Pluto, any **conjunction** or **parallel** can be favorable or unfavorable depending on the aspects Jupiter and Pluto receive from other planets.

Mental and Emotional Attributes and General Characteristics

Favorably Aspected	Unfavorably Aspected
Ability for abstract thought	Aggressive
Adaptable	Careless
Aspiration	Coarse
Athletic	Dictator
Benevolent	Dissipation
Broad minded	Dogmatic
Buoyant	Dull
Bold	Erroneous
Charitable	Exaggeration
Candid	Embezzlement
Compassionate	Excess
Concerned with the social welfare of others	Expansive Extravagant
Conservative	Fanatical
Courageous	Frank and outspoken
Decent	Impulsive
Devotional	Illicit
Dualistic	Inaccurate speech
Easy going	Indolent
Expansive	Indulgent
Executive ability	Lack of empathy
Exexecutive ability	Lavish
Intuition and hunches	Lawless
Fairness	Loud mouth
Freedom loving	Martyr
Good humored	Miscalculation
Good sport	Misjudgment
Good natured	Narrow minded
Honesty	Overextends
Hopeful	Overconfidence

Hospitable
Idealism
Independence
Integrity
Intelligent
Inspirational mentality
Jovial
Judicious
Just
Kind
Logical
Love of freedom
Loving
Loyalty
Lucky
Moral
Open minded
Optimistic
Popular
Polite
Peaceful
Philosophical
Pioneering spirit
Prophetic
Rational
Religious
Respect for law and order
Reverence
Seldom gets upset over petty details
Serene
Sincere
Sociable
Sound judgment
Straightforward
Studious
Successful
Truthful

Overindulgence in food and alcohol
Poor sport
Procrastination
Rebels against confinement and limitation
Reckless
Self esteem
Spendthrift
Showy
Sloppy
Rebellious
Tactless
Thriftless
Uncouth
Wanderlust
Wasteful

Favorably Aspected	Unfavorably Aspected

Vision
Versatile
Well balanced mentally
 and emotionally
Witty conversational

Jupiter's Rulership of People and Things

People	Things
Advisor	Academic
Advertising agent	Abundance
Airplane pilot	Advertising
Ambassador	Affluence
Animal breeder or trainer	Altar
Aristocrat	Bank
Attorney	Book
Banker	Book store
Bishop	benefit
Book publisher	Bonds
Broker	Charity
Brother-in-law	Church
Broadcast engineer	College
Clergyman	Commerce
Counselor	Correspondence course
Customs inspector	Courthouse
Diplomat	Dream
Doctor	Excessive
Educator	Expansion
Flight attendant	Foreign country
Foreigner	Horse
Friend	Increase and luck
Gambler	Law
Grandchild	Litigation
Guardian	Long trip
Horse breeder or trainer	Medal
Hunter	Occupation
In-law	Optimism
Interpreter	Orthodox religion

People	**Things**
Jockey	Orthodox religion
Judge	Parade
Lecturer	Publication
Legislator	Public expression of opinion
Lawyer	Philosophy
Lifeguard	Publishing company
Merchant	Race horse
Minister	Religion
Newspaper editor	Schooling
Official	Sports
Persons aged 45 to 60	Sporting equipment
Physician	Stables
Plutocrat	Visions
Pharmacist	Wager
Priest	Wealth
Priest	Winning
Philosopher	Protection
Physical education instructor	
Professor	
Prophet	
Psychologist	
Playground director	
Publicity director	
Public relations expert	
Sister-in-law	
Sportsman	
Stranger	
Student	
Teacher	
Tour guide	
Travel agent	
Traveling salesman	
Radar technician	
Radio announcer	
Telegraph and ship radio operators	
Uncle	
Younger brother	

People	Things
Welfare worker	
Individuals of different social levels	

Health
Blood poison
Blood disease
Blood problems such as high blood pressure
Diabetes and diseases caused through excess (overeating and drinking, etc.)
Claustrophobia
Boils
Disorders of the liver
Abscess
Hips
Jaundice
Liver
Low blood pressure
Thighs and accidents or ailments concerning them
Tumors
Sciatic nerve
Veins

Applying the Planetary Positions of Jupiter, Sagittarius and the Ninth House

Jupiter is the natural ruler of the ninth house and will convey its coloring to that house regardless of whether Sagittarius is on the ninth house cusp. This is one reason why individuals with the ruling planet of the Ascendant or the Sun, Moon, Venus or Mercury positioned in the ninth house are benevolent, compassionate, kind and loving.

Jupiter positioned in the first house adds the same qualities as those listed above to the individual's coloring. Sagittarius on the first house cusp also denotes sympathy, generosity and a philosophical outlook.

Any word from the llist of General Characteristics can be used if the aspects to Jupiter are favorable. If Jupiter should trine Saturn, for example, use words from the first columns under General Characteristics for Jupiter and Saturn. The individual with this aspect would have a rational mind (Jupiter) that is well disciplined (Saturn), combined with the ability to concentrate (Saturn). He also would be honest (Jupiter) and reliable (Saturn) in all his undertakings.

Do not underestimate the powers of Jupiter, for he can be just as troublesome as the heavier planets when afflicted.

For example, Jupiter in the second house of money in Virgo can be "penny wise and pound foolish" when badly aspected. Virgo is practical and earthy, Jupiter is expansive and fiery; on one hand they may check details (Mercury/Virgo) when spending on certain items and yet be extravagant (Jupiter) with other items.

The planet in aspect with Jupiter will disclose the individual or circumstances, according to the sign and house position, that will cause upsetting conditions concerning money.

Saturn's Role in the Universe

Saturn is ruler of the tenth house and Capricorn, which falls between December 22 and January 20 and is symbolized by the mountain goat.

It takes approximately 29 and one-half years for Saturn to travel through the 12 signs of the zodiac at the rate of two and one-half years per sign or one degree per month.

Saturn retrogrades once a year for a period of about 140 days and is stationary five days before and after retrogradation.

Saturn's nature is cardinal, earthy, cold, dry, masculine and barren.
Saturn is **exalted** in **Libra**
Has its **fall** in **Aries**
Is in its **detriment** in **Cancer**

Favorable Aspects

Favorable aspects to Saturn include **sextiles** and **trines** with all planets. No conjunction or parallel aspect with Saturn is considered favorable.

Unfavorable Aspects

Unfavoraable aspects to Saturn include **squares, oppositions, conjunctions** and **parallels** to all planets.

Mental and Emotional Attributes and General Characteristics

If Saturn or any other planet is positioned in Capricorn or the tenth house, its energies will naturally manifest through Capricorn or the tenth house matters listed in this chapter.

Favorably Aspected	**Unfavorably Aspected**
Actions well considered	Afraid
Ambition	Aggressive
Analysis	Aloof
Capacity for public career	Anxiety
Calm	Apathy
Caution	Apprehension
Common sense	Austerity
Chastity	Single minded drive for personal achievement
Conservative	
Concerned with prestige and reputation	Backward
	Begrudge
Cultural interests	Beamoan
Deliberate	Bitter
Determined	Calculating
Dignity	Callous
Diplomatic	Cold
Disciplined	Cruel
Discretion	Cynicism
Dogmatic	Desirous of controlling others
Dutiful	
Economical	Desirous of power
Endurance	Despair
Desirous of public prominence	Despondence
Detachment	Discontent
Faithful	Dissatisfaction
Firm	Domineering
Frugal	Doubt
Gravity	Destructive
Hard working	Emotional depression
Industrious	Envy
In-depth thought	Fear of loneliness
Integrity	Fear of rejection and failure

Favorably Aspected	**Unfavorably Aspected**
Justice	Fearfulness
Justful	Frigid
Methodical	Frustration
Needs and desires companionship	Friends chosen for usefulness
	Grasping
Organizational ability	Grievous
Likes to mingle with influential people or those with cultural backgrounds	Glum
	Grudge
	Hard
Preserving	Hardship
Persistence	Hatred
Political interests	Hostility
Practical	Insatiable ambition
Profound	Inhibition
Protective	Isolation
Prudent	Inferiority complex
Punctual	Inflexible
Self control and discipline	Intolerance
Self sacrificing	Jealousy
Sense of responsibility	Lacks humor
Seldom reacts with outward display of emotion	Lacks affection and tenderness
	Lacks adaptability
Serious	Lacks ability to relate to people and sympathize with them
Stability	
Strong sense of obligation	Loneliness
Strong willed	Limitation
Steadiness	Lust
Realistic	Malice
Reliability	Meanness
Reserved	Mercenary
Strength	Miserly
Shoulder responsibilities	Mistrustful
Tact	Malicious
Tenacious	Melancholy
Thrifty	Materialistic
Thoughtful	Obnoxious
Traditional	Opportunist

Favorably Aspected
Well directed energy
Very correct in manner and protocol
Saturn teaches through responsibility and restriction, and builds strength of character through adversity

Unfavorably Aspected
Overly conventional
Peevish
Pessimistic
Reclusive
Relentless
Resentful
Revenge
Rigid
Ruthless
Sadistic
Self centered
Selfish
Secretive
Severe
Self pity
Snobbery
Sordid
Stubborn
Shy
Slow
Social climber
Suspicion
Takes advantage of others' weaknesses
Unbending
Unforgiving
Unemotional
Unsociable
Unsympathetic
Uses others as a stepping stones to success
Vindictive
Work and responsibility come before emotional and sexual fulfillment

People and Things

People
Aged person
Administrator
Architect
Agriculturist
Boss
Brick layer
Brick maker
Builder
Carpenter
Chiropractor
Civil engineer
Civil service worker
Civil lawyer
Construction worker
Coal miner
Dictator
Executive
Farm worker
Father
FBI agent
Food handler
Hard laborer
Gardener
Governor
Hotelier
Housekeeper
Industrial engineer
Janitor
Landlord
Leather worker
Manager
Mason
Miner
Mining engineer
Mathemetician
Mayor

Things
Ambition
Atrophy
Attic, cellar and all dark places
Austere
Bankrupt
Bereavement
business district
Career
Cove
Calamity
Cement
Cemetery
Cellar
Clay
Credit
Change (slow to develop, but long lasting)
Calendar
Clock
Church yard
Chamber of commerce
City hall
Chronic condition
Clay
Corpse
Business affairs
Debt
Depression
Deprivation
Disaster
Dishonor
Dclay
Fear
fences and fenced areas
Foundation
Frigid

People	Things
Monarch	Funeral
Manager	Establishment
Miser	Excavation
Monk	Government
Man of authority	Grave
Man from the past	Granite
Old and past conditions	Honor
Old friends	Hill
Older people	Hindrance
Osteopath	Inhibition
Parent	Justice
Person of prestigious background	Laborious job
	Land
Person of integrity and honor	Lead
Person of authority	Leather goods
Personnel worker	Limitation
People aged 60 to 70	Loss
Plasterer	Melancholy
Plumber	Misfortune
Potter	Mortgage
Politician	Mortuary
President	Mountain area
Purchasing agent	Mine
Real estate broker	Nunnery
Repairman	Obligation
Scientist	Obstacle
Shoemaker	Obstruction
Shepherd	Office
Spinster	Organizations
Stockbroker	Open country
Superior	Past condition
Tilers and plasterers	Position
Time keeper	Poverty
Undertaker	Profession or trade
Vocational counselor	Prisons
Watch and clock repairman	Real estate
Watchman (night)	Responsibility

People
Widows and widowers
Municipal workers and those paid by taxpayer money, such as city administrators, politicians, city and state employees, teachers, police officers, firefighters, garbage collectors and water meter readers.
Those living a life of seclusion or austerity such as monks, hermits, nuns and misers.

Things
Restriction
Rock
Rocky places
Rank and reputation
Refrigeration, morgues and all places that are cold
Sorrow
Stone
Stagnation
Serious
Tardy
Time
Thrifty
Tragedy
Vault

Health
Arthritis
Cancer
Cold
Blood clot
Deafness and hearing problems
Dentures
Dull aches and pains
Fatigue
Bony structure of the body and its ailments
Frigidity or inhibitions in sexual expression
Gall stones
Joints
Hair
Hypochondria
Hardening of the arteries
Knees
Ligaments
Rheumatism
Skin
Teeth

Toothache
Tuberculosis

Applying the Planetary Positions of Saturn, Capricorn and the Tenth House

Many astrologers have a dire view of Saturn. However, even with such aspects as squares, parallels, conjunctions and oppositions, one can overcome the heaviness of Saturn through a thorough understanding of its energy.

Saturn represents restriction, limitation, hindrance, responsibility and a deep sense of obligation. This manifests through an individual or circumstances represented by the house and sign position of the planet squaring Saturn and the house and sign position of Saturn plus the houses they rule.

If, for example, Saturn squares a planet in the sixth house of work and service to others, at some time the will work out the potentials listed of the sixth house through various circumstances and individuals. The native with this Saturn (ruler of bosses) placement may one day be supervised by a superior who will sense that the individual takes his obligations (Saturn) seriously and handles each task with attention to detail (Mercury/Virgo/sixth house). This supervisor may impose upon the individual with highly difficult tasks or by requiring laborious hours. The native may quietly assume the added burden because he feels responsible for it, or may feel that no one else is as capable of handling these tasks as he.

There is nothing wrong with assuming responsibility, but if one is being taken advantage of, then he must recognize the fact and learn to stand up to his boss and refuse the extra burdens. However, astrologers know this is seldom done because the square aspect seems to embed a strong guilt complex that erroneously ties the native to his (or what he feels is his) sense of responsibility.

Since the sixth house also rules aunts and uncles, it is possible one of them may make the native feel a sense of obligation, possibly by buying him gifts he cannot use in order to receive favors or errands in return. It also could be something else that ties the native to his aunt or uncle through a sense of responsibility. The native must recognize the action that this square with Saturn imparts and handle the situation accordingly. Otherwise an eventual feeling of resentment and frustration will prevail towards the aunt or uncle.

As the sixth house also rules small pets and animals, children in the family may request a pet; but it will be the native who has Saturn square a planet in the sixth house that will assume responsibility for its health and care. However, if the planet in the sixth house receives favorable aspects from other planets, the native will not object to this added responsibility. Nevertheless, pets will always seem to require extra care due to possible chronic health problems.

The house in which Saturn is positioned indicates where the native must learn to accept responsibility and the fulfillment of duties. With an afflicted Saturn, he must learn when to draw the line on responsibility or he will begin to resent the person or circumstance curtailing him.

Uranus' Role in the Universe

Uranus is ruler of the eleventh house and Aquarius, which falls between January 21 and February 19 and is symbolized by the water bearer.

It takes approximately 84 years for Uranus to travel through the 12 signs of the zodiac at the rate of seven years per sign, four and one-half degrees per year or one minute per day.

Uranus retrogrades for approximately five months and is stationary about five days before and after retrogradation.

Uranus nature is airy, fixed, cold, dry, positive, masculine and barren.

Uranus is **exalted** in **Scorpio**
Has its **fall** in **Taurus**
Is in its **detriment** in **Leo**

Favorable Aspects

Favorable asepcts to Uranus include sextiles and trines with all planets. No conjunction or parallel aspect with Uranus is considered favorable.

Unfavorable Aspects

Unfavorable aspects to Uranus include squares and oppositions to all planets as well as conjunctions and parallels with all planets.

Mental and Emotional Attributes and General Characteristics

Favorably Aspected	Unfavorably Aspected
Action	Absentminded
Advanced in thought	Abnormal
Adventurous	Aggressive
Altruistic	Antisocial
Amiable	Abnormal aversion
Articulate	Bizarre activities
Authority	Compulsive liar
Cheerful	Contrary
Considerate	Cold
Compassionate	Crank
Clairvoyant	Deals with impractical schemes
Conversationalist (current events, discoveries)	Defiant
	Detached
Cooperative	Deviation
Creative	Destructive
Curiosity	Dictator
Diplomatic	Disorder
Electric	Disruptive
Excellent	Eccentric
Faithful	Erratic behavior
Feeling	Exaggerates
Friendly	Fanaticism
Generous	Free spirited
Genius	Hostile
Gentle	Inaccurate in speech
Gets along well with people from different backgrounds	Intolerant
	Impractical
Humanitarian	Inconsistent
Idealistic	Irresponsible
Ingenious	Impatient
Insight	Lack of tact
Intelligent	Lawless
Intuitive	Licentious
Inventive	Meddlesome
Imaginative	Morbid fantasy

Favorably Aspected	**Unfavorably Aspected**
Interested in the betterment of mankind	Nervous irritability
Inspirational	Neuroses and delusions
Ipersonal	Nonconformist
Independent	Notorious
Love of debate (exchange of ideas)	Overly talkative
Love of freedom	Peculiar
Magnetism	Perverse
Mechanical ability	Rebellious
Modern	Shocks others through sadistic or unusual statements or actions
Natural rebel	Slovenly
Original	Strange
Politically and socially minded	Unconventional
Positive	Unsympathetic
Progressive	Untidy
Pleasant	
Reformer	
Romantic	
Sociable	
Susceptible to flattery	
Strong likes and dislikes	
Self-reliant	
Self-willed	
Tolerant	
Traditional standards not always observed	
Unconventional	
Versatile	
Visionary	
Vulnerable	

People and Things

People	**Things**
Actor	Aeronautics
Actress	Accident
Acquaintance	Association

People	Things
Advisor	Adultery
Auto mechanic	Air travel
Aviator	Abortion
Aerospace technician	Art store
Aeronautical engineer	Airplane
Astrologer	Automobile
Astronomer	Automobile dealer
Composer	Airplane hanger
Counselor	Aura
Computer operator	Bereavement
Discoverer	Bizarre
Electrician	Club
Electrical fixture salesman	Congress
Electrical engineer	Crisis
Electronic technician	Catastrophe
Free spirited person	CB, TV and radiosystems
Friend	Defiance
Genius	Disorder
Government official	Disruptive
Humanitarian	Fluctuation
Hypnotist	Disaster
Inventor	Divorce
Lecturer	Dynamite
Musician	ESP
Metaphysician	Explosives
Nonconformist	Electronics
Nuclear physicist	Electrical appliance
Numerologist	Earthquake
Odd people	Furniture store
Pervert	Frenzy
People aged 70 to 85	Group creativity
People difficult to understand	Group activity
Physician	House of Commons
Programmer	Hopes and wishes
Psychologist	Magnet
Radio or TV announcer	Miscarriage
Radio or TV technician	New idea

People	**Things**
Radiologist	Occult
Reformer	Occupation that is unique, uncommon or different
Researcher	Organization
Revolutionary	Outlaw
Old conditions that suddenly direction	Pervert
Scientist	Perversion
change and take a new	Premature
Social worker	Partings
Statesman	Public catastrophe
Stranger	Radium
Space physicist	Romance
Technician	Separation
Teacher	Spasmodic conditions
Those who break new ground or have unconentional ideas	Shock
	Sudden, unexpected event
Those with power and authority over others (ruler, chief of staff, anarchist, etc.)	Sudden change
	Severing of ties
	Social reform
Writer	That which is bizarre
X-ray technician	Thunderbolts, lightning, storms, tornados, hurricanes and other acts of God
	Traveler
	Tragedy
	Upset
	Unconventional
	X-Ray film and machine

Uranus' Rulership Over Health

Abortion
Ankles
Accidents
Circulatory system
Cramps in the calves
Health condition requiring X-ray or electrical shock treatment
Illegitimacy

Injury
Incurable disease
Intuitive intellect
Miscarriage
Nervous spasm or twitch
Nervous system
Operation
Paralysis
Physical change
Sexual perversion
Spasmodic pain
Sudden death
Sudden nervous breakdown

Applying the Planetary Positions of Uranus, Aquarius and the Eleventh House

An individual, for example, with Uranus positioned in the tenth house of career would not be happy with a run of the mill job. Only those which are unique or different would be appealing or interesting. Often these individuals may hold jobs in which the hours vary from the norm such as working days one week and nights the next or working two weeks with the next off.

Uranus in the tenth house creates something different in either the vocation or the working conditions, and because of its position these variations are the thing that draws the native to that type of work.

Because Uranus also rules aeronautics, automobiles, electrical systems, and TV and radio, these are possible career choice.

Notice the words disruptive and sudden change in the lists; this may occur on the job. Either the native becomes bored with his position and suddenly quits, or the boss makes spasmodic changes in the job or department.

Aquarius on the tenth house cusp gives the same effect on career.

If Aquarius is on the second house of money, one may have unique or different ideas as to how money should be spent or earned and, as Aquarius is a fixed sign, the native may try to impose his ideas on others. Aquarius also causes fluctuation in finances, bringing years of plenty and followed by years of lean.

These are a few examples of Aquarius on the second house of

money. Other characteristics are identified by applying the words in the lists to money, finances and moveable possessions.

Neptune's Role in the Universe

Neptune is ruler of the twelfth house and Pisces, which falls between February 20 and March 19 and is symbolized by the fishes.

It takes approximately 165 years for Neptune to travel through the 12 signs of the zodiac at the rate of 14 years per sign or two degrees per year.

Neptune retrogrades for approximately five months and is stationary about five days before and after retrogradation.

Neptune's nature is mutable, watery, moist, warm, feminine and fruitful.

Neptune is **exalted** in **Leo**
Has its **fall** in **Aquarius**
Is in its **detriment** in **Virgo**

Favorable Aspects

Favorable aspects to Neptune include sextiles and trines with all planets, as well as conjunctions and parallels with Venus and Jupiter.

Unfavorable Aspects

Unfavorable aspects to Neptune include squares and oppositions to all planets as well as conjunctions and parallels with Mars, Saturn and Uranus.

Doubtful Aspects

Doubtful aspects to Neptune include conjunctions and parallels with the Sun, Moon, Mercury and Pluto, which can be good or bad depending on the aspects to the conjunctions or parallels.

Mental and Emotional Attributes and General Characteristics

Favorably Aspected	Unfavorably Aspected
Adaptability	Abnormal behavior
Affectionate	Absentminded
Altruistic	Alcoholism
Artistic	Chaotic mentality
Awareness of higher states of consciousness	Delusions
	Depression caused by slights or ill-stated remarks
Broadminded	
Clairvoyant	Dislikes physical work
Compassionate	Dishonest
Considerate	Demanding
Creative	Disorganized
Devotion	Distraught
Desire for solitude	Dreamer of unrealized dreams
Dreamy	Drug addiction
Empathy	Ego needs constant reassurance
Emotional	Easily led and influenced
Exceptional	Extremes of temperament
Fanciful	Escapism
Feels and senses rather than reasons	Elusive
	Foul tempered
Friendly	Fraud
Generous	Frustration through minor worries
Gentle	
Glamour	Gullible
Good promoter	Hallucination
Gregarious	Hypersensitive
Idealistic	Hyperemotional
Imaginative	Hysterical
Impressionable	Illusion
Inspirational	Indecisive

Favorably Aspected	Unfavorably Aspected
Intuitive	Indulgence
Loving	Inferiority complex
Lover of peace and harmony	Intangible
Loyal	Impractical
Meditation brings peace of mind	Immaterial
Mediumistic	Incomprehensible
Molds groups of people or orgnaizations	Instable
	Inability to rationalize
Mysticism	Insecure
Passionate	Lack of will power
Poetic	Lazy
Prefers working quietly and clandestinely	Love of luxury
	Magnifies slights or problems
Prophetic ability	Difficulty separating real from unreal
Psychic awareness	
Refined thoughts and ideas	Martyr
Receptive	Makes extravagant statements
Seeks the ideal	Malice
Sentimental	Moody
Spiritual aspirations	Mental confusion
Spiritual in expression and thought	Morbid imagination
	Misrepresentation
Sensitive	Nagger
Subtle	Narcotic
Sympathetic	Negative thinking
Tender	Obsession
Tolerant of others	Overactive imagination
Tranquil	Paranoid
Unselfish	Perverse
Vibrates with excitement	Possessive
Visionary	Pretentious
Vulnerable to surrounding conditions	Promiscuous
	Secret involvement and intrigue
Warm	Self indulgence
Witty	Self deception
Works well with emotionally disturbed or handicapped	Sensuality
	Schemes

Favorably Aspected	Unfavorably Aspected
people	Subtlety
	Strange or unnatural desires and appetites
	Split personality
	Strange fears
	Self destructive
	Self imposed isolation
	Self pity
	Sexual excess and variety
	Solitude vs. need for others
	Susceptible to depression
	Swindle
	Treacherous
	Unreliable intuitions
	Uncertainty
	Vacillating
	Vague
	Weird feelings
	Worrisome
	Promotion of schemes to gain money without working for it
	Wrong feelings or intuition interferes with making sound decisions
	Emotional insecurity

People and Things

People	Things
Abnormal person	Adoration
Accomplice	Alibi
Actor	Anesthetic
Actress	Alcohol
Addict	Beach
Artist	Bewilder
Bartender	Biology
Bigamist	Blackmail
Biologist	Bribery

People	**Things**
Chain store manager	Behind the scenes acitivty
Chemist	Business merger
Chemical engineer	Chaos
Clandestine relationship	Charity
Cocktail waitress	Confusion
Cosmetician	Conspiracy
Crazy person	Communal living
Deceitful person	Creativity
Doctor	Chain store
Druggist	Crime
Drunkard	Criminal
Dubious person	Confidential matter
Dancer	Dancing
Diver	Deception
Dreamer	Detective and investigative work
Detective	Delusions
Diplomat	Disappointment
Fashion designer	Distillery
Fisherman	Dream
Hospital attendant	Dualistic
Healer	ESP
Impostor	Fishing tackle and equipment
Member of religious sect	Fraud
Monk	Gas meter
Make-up artist	Gas appliance
Movie director	Gas system
Market research analyst	Gas and gasoline
Mobs and popular movements	Hallucinations
Medium	Heroin, LSD and related drugs
Musician	Hospitals
Nun	Inability to see matters in proper perspective
Nurse	Infatuation
Nurse	Institution
Occultist	Isolation
Oceanographer	Inspiration
Oil field worker	Jail
Parapsychologist	

People	**Things**
Peculiar person	Liquid
Pharmacist	Limitation
Priest	Maritime matter
Psychic	Misrepresentation
Psychiatrist	Manufacturer of footwear
Religious worker	Movie
Spiritual leader	Music
Seaman	Nightmare
Secret enemy	Nigh club
Secret agent	Occult
Shipping merchant	Occupations connected withil shipping, fishing and water
Shoemaker	
Shoe salesman	Oil
Spy	Obsession
Social worker	Paint
Social wo	Perfume
Religious worker	Performing arts
Teacher	Petroleum product
Those with negative attitude	Poetry
Trickster	Poorhouse
Trickster	Prison
Visionary	Plot
Wine merchant	Privacy
Substitutes such as foster parents, or step-brothers or sisters	Promotional work
	Promotion
	Poison
	Psychic center
	Psychic healing
	Psychic influence
	Premonition
	Restaurant
	Restriction
	Romance and emotion
	Secret sorrows and self inflicted solitude
	Scheme
	Stream

People

Things
Secrecy
Scandal
Secret matter
Secret society or organization
Seduction
Sea
Singing
Suicide
Swimming
Tobacco
Travel by plane or boat
Trance
TV and radio
Unreality
Water
Weird feelings and experiences
Workhouse

Health
Anemia
Bisexuality
Coma or comatose state
Deformity
Dentures
Eye glasses
Feet and related problems
Glass eye
Hearing aid
Irrational fear
Inferiority complex
Mental and nervous condition
Psychosomatic illness
Illness difficult to diagnose or detect
Illness resulting from animal or insect bites or stings
Illness resulting from overindulgence in drugs or alcohol
Wasting diseases
Infection

Poisoning
Prostheses
Sensitivity to anesthesia
Sensitivity to certain drugs
Sensitivity to alcohol
Toes, bunions, corns and related problems

Applying the Planetary Positions of Neptune, Pisces and the Twelfth House

Neptune is perhaps the most difficult planet to understand because of its subtle and illusionary energy.

As an example, Neptune is placed in the first house to view its influence on the Ascendant. If well aspected, expect artistic or creative ability, and the native will be compassionate, considerate, desirous of solitude, emotional and sensitive. He may enjoy fishing, swimming, dancing, singing, music or long walks in the woods, because any of the above mentioned activities act as a form of escapism or mild tranquilizer, releasing all inner tensions and leaving the native relaxed and feeling at one with the universe.

However, if Neptune also receives unfavorable aspects, the native must guard against alcoholism, deception, day dreaming and being easily lead or influenced by others.

Pisces on the third house cusp often colors the individual as a day dreamer or one who builds castles in the air. The same native is secretive about his thoughts (Mercury/third house) but can be mentally creative.

As the third house rules brothers and sisters, there may be a secret concerning one of them or they may have foster brothers or sisters, depending upon the natal placement of Neptune, its sign, house position and aspects it receives.

Venus conjunct Neptune may stir a secret (Neptune) desire for a romantic affair (Venus). This conjunction also endows an altruistic nature, making the native extremely sensitive to the needs of others.

Pluto's Role in the Universe

Pluto is ruler of the eighth house and Scorpio. Scorpio falls between October 23 and November 21 and is symbolized by the Scorpion.

Pluto requires about 248 years to travel through the 12 signs of the zodiac for its speed varies greatly and ranges from 14 to 25 years in one sign (average of 10 degrees per year).

Pluto is in retrograde motion about five months of the year. Its stationary period varies from 12 to 19 days before and after retrogradation.

Pluto's nature is fixed, watery moist, cold, feminine and fruitful.
Is in its **detriment** in **Taurus**
Its exalatation and fall have not yet been determined

Favorable Aspects

Favorable Aspects to Pluto include sextiles and trines with all planets. No conjunction or parallel aspect with Pluto is considered favorable, although some are listed under the doubtful heading.

Unfavorable Aspects

Unfavorable aspects to Pluto include squares and oppositions to all planets, as well as conjunctions and parallels (except those listed as doubtful).

Doubtful Aspects

Doubtful aspects between Pluto and the Sun, Moon, Mercury, Venus, Jupiter and Neptune are conjunctions and parallels. They can be favorable or unfavorable depending upon the aspects Pluto and the above planets receive from the other planets.

Mental and Emotional Attributes and General Characteristics

Favorably Aspected	Unfavorably Aspected
Ability to handle difficult and disagreeable tasks	Adulterous
	Adulterate
Ability to overcome bad habits and faults	Always on the defensive
	Aloof
Assumes position of trust and responsibility	Bold
	Calculating
Change and transformation	Callous
Complex nature (outwardly calm, inwardly tense)	Contemptuous
	Cold
Decisive	Corrupt
Determined	Courageous
Egoistic	Cold
Emotions run deep and strong	Critical
Energetic	Cruel
Fiercely possessive	Cunning
Frank	Debauchery
Good luck	Deceit
Honorable	Defiance
Inispires strength and faith	Degradation
Intense	Depravity
Intensely loyal	Desirous of power
Interested in mysteries of life and death	Destructive
	Deviltry
Loyal	Dishonor
Natural healer	Extremes of passion
Organizational and planning skills	Extremely tense
	Fanatical
Outward expression of calmness regardless of	Feeds on weakness of others
	Indecent

Favorably Aspected	**Unfavorably Aspected**
inner feelings	Frigid or sexually inhibited
Loyal	Ill luck
Natural healer	Immoralt
Organizational and planning skills	Impulsive
Perfection	Indifferent
Psychic receptivity	Internalizes self
Possessive	Intense likes and dislikes
Frigid or sexually inhibited	Incapable of expressing love
Religious	Jealous
Reserved	Lawless
Restless probing mind	Liar
Renewal	Lustful
Rourcefulness	Obscene
Rejuvenation	Perverted
Regeneration	Power wielding
Spirituality	Possessive
Secretive with personal and financial affairs	Passionate
Self-controlled	Relentless
Strong loyalty	Sarcasm
Shrewd	Seduction
Sympathy with masses of people	Selfish
Suspicious	Skeptical
Traditional	Sinister
Willfulness	Shrewd
Persuasive leader	Suspicious
Superhuman	Sensual
	Sexually abuse
	Secretive
	Stubborn
	Temper
	Temperamental
	Treachery
	Underhandedness
	Unscrupulous
	Unsympathetic
	Vindictiveness
	Violent

Favorably Aspected	Unfavorably Aspected
	Vulgar
	Willful
	Unyielding

People and Things

People	Things
Archeologist	Alimony
Athletic manager	Alias
Assassin	Alibi
Bail bondsman	Ambush
Banker	Anonymous
Bill collector	Atomic energynonymous
Butcher	Change that ends one phase of
Computer programmer	life and leads to another
Convict	Cave
Coroner	Cesspool
Corpse	Contamination
Corporation executive	Coercion
Dentist	Creative faculties
Detective	Crematory
Dictator	Crime and police activity
Embalmer	Death and things of the dead
Faith healer	Decay
Funeral director	Disaster
Gangster	Embalming
Gynecologist	Eliminate
Hoodlum	ESP
Insurance adjuster	Grave
Insurance agent	Healing power
IRS agent	Inheritance
Kidnaper	Insurance
Large groups or masses of	Insurance claim
people	Industrial real estate
Liquor dealer	Joint finances
Mafia member	Legacy
Magician	Life hereafter
Market research analyst	Magic

People
Medical technician
Mortician
Organized labor leader
Plumber
Physician
Police officer
Politician
Propagandist
Prostitute
Psychiatrist
Psychic healer
Racketeer
Researcher
Religious leader
Satan
Spy
Seducer
Spiritualist
Statistician
Surgeon
Secret investigator
Technician
Transformer
Troubleshooter
Terrorist
Terrorist
Underground crime syndicator

Things
Medical office
Mine
Military affairs
Morgue
Money belonging to others
Murder
Mortgage
Nuclear medicine
Nuclear weapon
Ordeal
Pollution
Police activity
Operation
Prostitution
Rape
Radio
Partner's money
Public's money
Pension
Rebirth
Regeneration
Reincarnation
Research
Spirituality
Secret orders and sexual societies
Slaughter house
Subconscious
Surgery
Sex orgy
Space flight
Suicide
Subway
Sexual gratification
Swamp
Stagnant water
Taxes
TV

People

Things
Treachery
Will and testament

Health
AIDS
Bladder disorder
Bladder infection
Blood poisoning
Constipation
Groin
Genital disorder
Generative system and disease
Hemorrhoids
Prostate glands
Procreative urge
Rectum
Recuperative power
Sexual energy
Sex organs
Sexual hang-ups
Tapeworm
Toxemia
Veneral disease

Applying the Planetary Positions of Pluto, Scorpio and the Eighth House

Pluto is the planet of change and reformation. Because these changes take place slowly and gradually, the effects are not at all like those of Uranus, which is eruptive or sudden. It is more like climbing the stairs with each step bringing the native to a different level.

If, for example, Pluto is positioned in the first house, the native goes through a series of changes that affect his general circumstances or welfare such as being drafted or moving to another city. Pluto in the first house also will affect the native's attitude toward others and the general state of appearance: the native will begin to make gradual changes in the style of dress, hair coloring or styling or removal of a facial blemish on the face.

In whatever house Pluto is located, change or reformation will be experienced within that area of life and through the individuals represented by that house.

Pluto is also the dictator and if unfavorably aspected, its house position discloses who will try to dictate to the native. If in the fifth house, for example, children may attempt to boss the native; in the seventh, the marriage partner; or in the first, the native is the dictator and will not stand being bossed by others.

If Mercury is trine Pluto, the aspect can indicate an individual who is shrewd in his thinking and knows how to ferret out information without revealing any of his own. This is an excellent placement for a salesman (Mercury) along the lines of insurance (Pluto) or any field that deals with money belonging to others such as lotteries, mortgages or banking.